For unto us a child is born,
unto us a son is given: and His
name shall be called
Wonderful,
Counsellor,
The Mighty God,
The Everlasting Father,
The Prince of Peace.

Written by
Lance Douglas

And it came to pass in those days, that there went out a decree from Caesar Augustus, that all the world should be taxed. And all went to be taxed, every one into his own city. And Joseph and Mary went up from Galilee, out of the city of Nazareth, into the city of David, which is called Bethlehem, to be taxed; with Mary, his wife, being great with child.

The little town of Bethlehem,
Had grown dark and the
lights were dim.
A stable was Joseph's only choice,
No room was made for Him.

The ox and the donkey from the stable have significant symbolism in ancient Israel. The ox is symbolic of "patience" and "steadiness." The donkey is symbolic of "humility" and "readiness to serve."

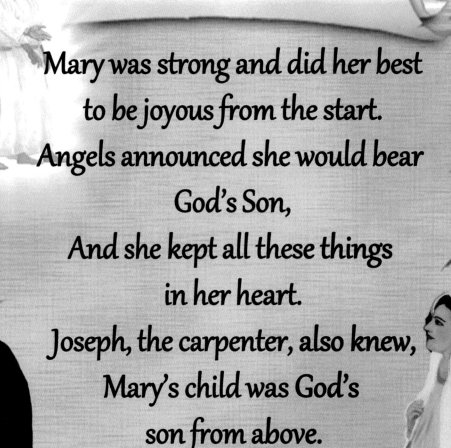

Mary was strong and did her best
to be joyous from the start.
Angels announced she would bear
God's Son,
And she kept all these things
in her heart.
Joseph, the carpenter, also knew,
Mary's child was God's
son from above.
He wondered if he had done
all he could,
To prepare for this gift of love.

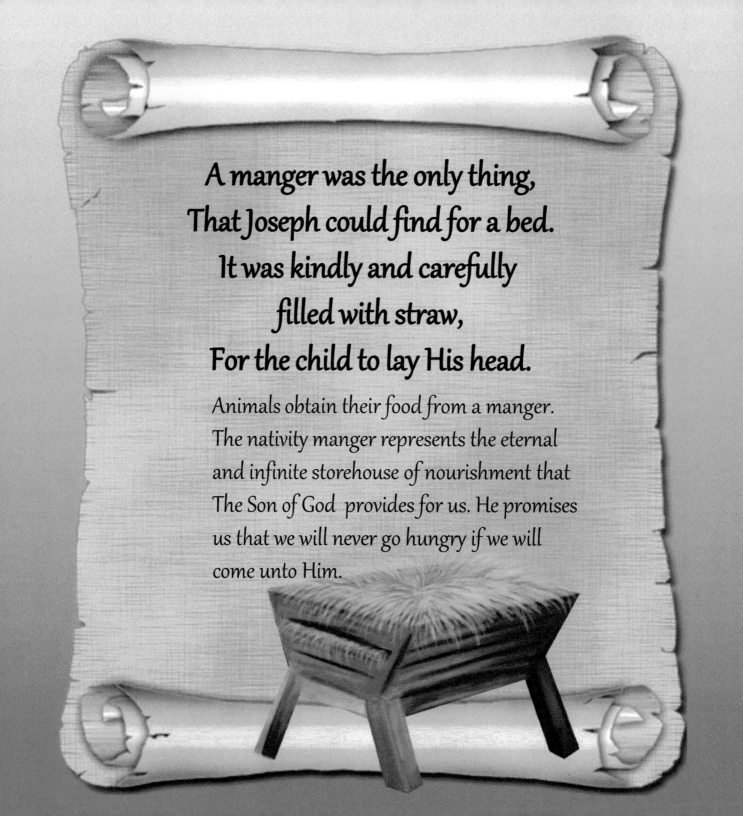

A manger was the only thing,
That Joseph could find for a bed.
It was kindly and carefully
filled with straw,
For the child to lay His head.

Animals obtain their food from a manger.
The nativity manger represents the eternal
and infinite storehouse of nourishment that
The Son of God provides for us. He promises
us that we will never go hungry if we will
come unto Him.

Mary brought forth her firstborn son,
And swaddled him in a blanket of white.
The heavens rejoiced at the wondrous news,
The Savior was born that night!

The significance of the baby Jesus' "swaddling clothes"
is often overlooked. The angels specifically explained
to the shepherds that "swaddling clothes" would
be "a sign" to them that the baby was the "Saviour,
which is Christ the Lord."

Being wrapped in swaddling clothes is
also symbolic of Jesus being the
true son of David.

A new star appeared in the
dark night sky,
Announcing the child's birth.
As promised, a Savior had
been born,
To save all who lived on earth.

In the darkness of the night sky, God placed
a new star in the heavens declaring that
the Light of the World had arrived. Thus,
God chose light as a symbol to represent
His Only Begotten Son. And now, Christmas
"lights" help us to remember the light from the
star of Bethlehem.

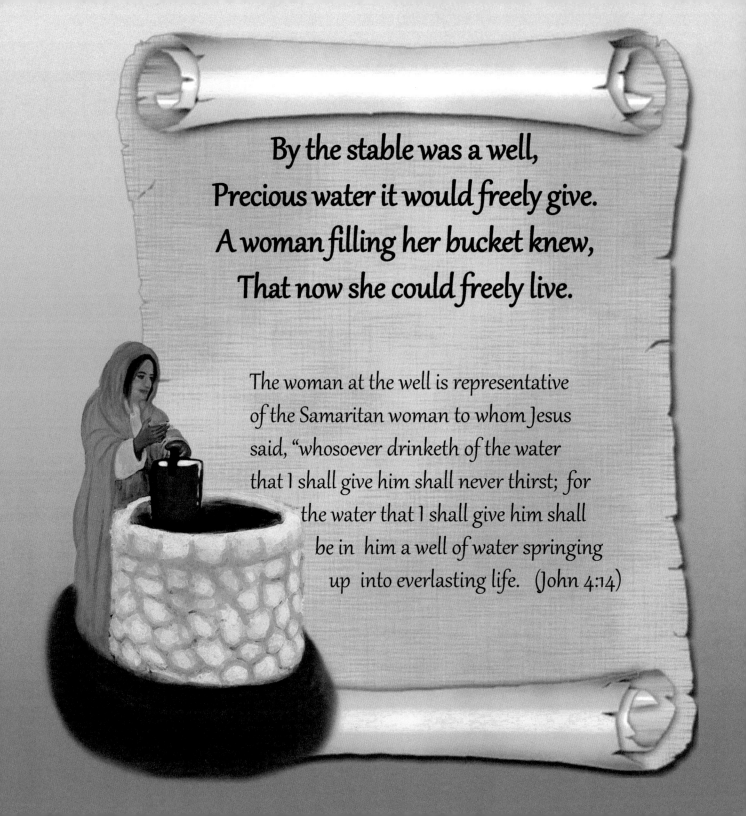

By the stable was a well,
Precious water it would freely give.
A woman filling her bucket knew,
That now she could freely live.

The woman at the well is representative
of the Samaritan woman to whom Jesus
said, "whosoever drinketh of the water
that I shall give him shall never thirst; for
the water that I shall give him shall
be in him a well of water springing
up into everlasting life. (John 4:14)

Shepherds were watching their
flocks by night,
When angels suddenly appeared.
"Good tidings of great joy"
The angels declared,
And the shepherds no longer feared.

Jesus came as the Lamb of God to die for the sins of the world. It was only fitting that the first announcement that the Lamb of God had been born would be proclaimed by heavenly messengers to the humble shepherds keeping watch over their flocks in the hills near Bethlehem.

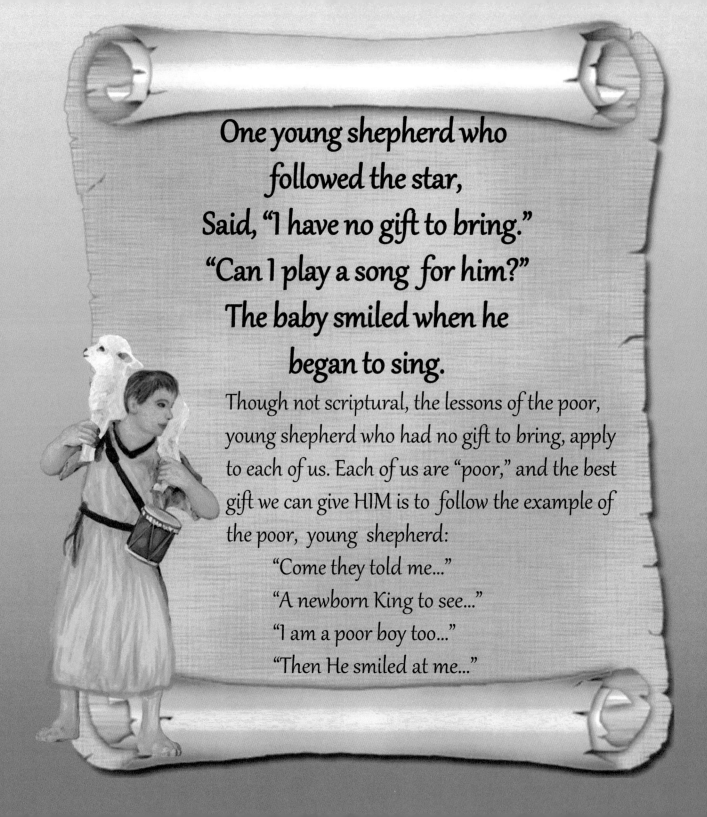

One young shepherd who
followed the star,
Said, "I have no gift to bring."
"Can I play a song for him?"
The baby smiled when he
began to sing.

Though not scriptural, the lessons of the poor,
young shepherd who had no gift to bring, apply
to each of us. Each of us are "poor," and the best
gift we can give HIM is to follow the example of
the poor, young shepherd:

"Come they told me..."

"A newborn King to see..."

"I am a poor boy too..."

"Then He smiled at me..."

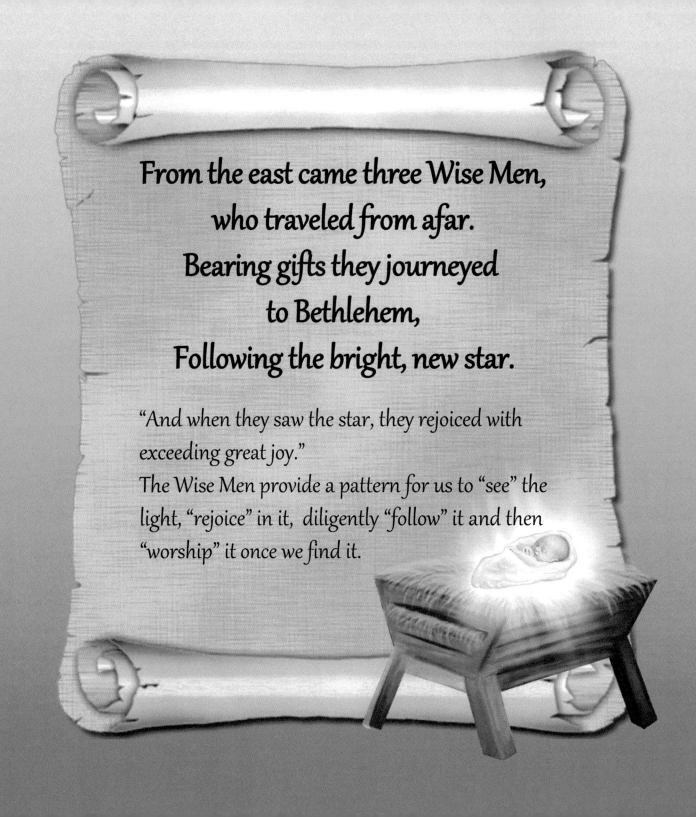

From the east came three Wise Men,
who traveled from afar.
Bearing gifts they journeyed
to Bethlehem,
Following the bright, new star.

"And when they saw the star, they rejoiced with exceeding great joy."
The Wise Men provide a pattern for us to "see" the light, "rejoice" in it, diligently "follow" it and then "worship" it once we find it.

The first Wise Man brought gold,
a treasure made for a king.
He placed the treasure
by the manger,
As heavenly choirs began to sing.

Gold is a symbol of royalty. It
represents the divine royalty
of the Christ Child.

The second Wise Man brought frankincense,
Fragrant and glowing with light.
A special gift for the Christ Child,
The Holy One born that night.

Frankincense is a resin obtained from a tree. It is highly fragrant when it is burned in worship as an offering to God, symbolizing holiness and righteousness.

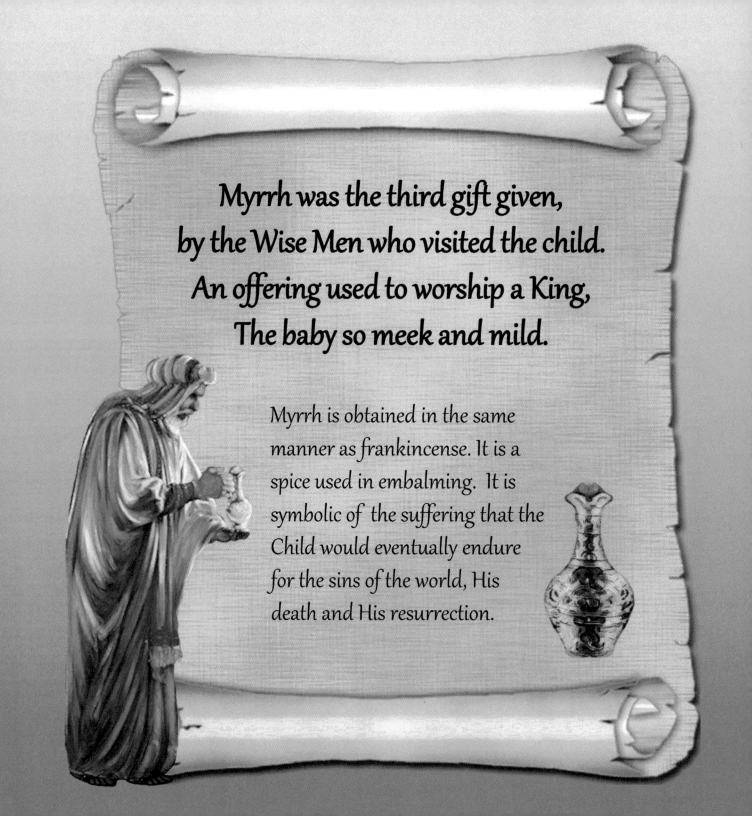

Myrrh was the third gift given,
by the Wise Men who visited the child.
An offering used to worship a King,
The baby so meek and mild.

Myrrh is obtained in the same
manner as frankincense. It is a
spice used in embalming. It is
symbolic of the suffering that the
Child would eventually endure
for the sins of the world, His
death and His resurrection.

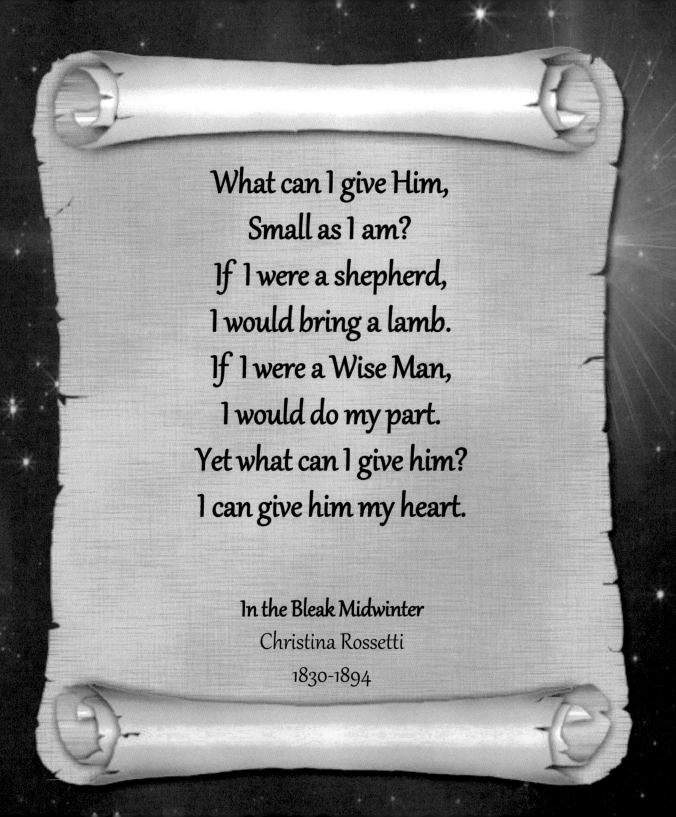

What can I give Him,
Small as I am?
If I were a shepherd,
I would bring a lamb.
If I were a Wise Man,
I would do my part.
Yet what can I give him?
I can give him my heart.

In the Bleak Midwinter

Christina Rossetti

1830-1894

Oh come let us adore him.
CHRIST the LORD!

Made in the USA
Middletown, DE
15 August 2019